Mangoes and Other Things: The Adventures of Two Loved-up Losers

Chloe Young Kobe Tong

BookLeaf Publishing

Presentation by *BookLeaf Publishing*

Web: www.bookleafpub.com

E-mail: info@bookleafpub.com

ISBN: 9789357690331

First edition 2022

For all the boring and sensible couples of the world.

PREFACE

How does a chance, tipsy meeting at a Covent Garden bar meander its way to a flailing punt at poetry stardom? We have no idea either.

Side by side

Trying new things is scary,
But with you,
I am up for any adventure.
You make me:
Braver,
Bolder,
Stronger,
Greater than I thought I'd ever be.
I hope you feel half as safe as me.

We are each other's champions,
The tough times
Never seem as hard when we face them hand in
hand.
Food, heights, cars and more,
Nothing seems unconquerable,
Too mighty,
Too fierce,
Too frightening,
Together.

Pinballs

Lady Luck's a lier, I know it's true,
But maybe Fate's real, all down to you

A pinball machine shook side to side,
Two silver ball bearings rattling by,
Dinging off walls and levers and traps,
Dodging the holes and pinging off flaps,
A metally blur scribbles in a flash,
The two flying missiles impossibly clash,
The most improbable collision,
So likely to miss, so hard to envision

Like throwing paint at a wall,
And it makes Starry Night,
Playing Scrabble blindfolded,
And it writes Wuthering Heights,
Tapping away at your desk,
And it plays Stairway to Heaven,
Chucking your rubbish away,
And it builds a Rolls-Royce engine

Somehow, somewhere,
Somewhen, somewhy,
Amid the chaos of,
The pinball machine of life,

There emerged you and I,
Two wild pinging pinballs rattling by,
Now forever side by side

Mangoes, and other things

If I go in the Aygo to take a kilo of mangoes
home,
Then a man goes with mangoes,
But a man who knows mangoes,
Knows mangoes are no-gos in tacos.
For as far as we know,
And as far as it goes,
There's zero tacos with a kilo of mangoes.
Mayo, yes, and a glass of vino,
But even in gyros mangoes don't go.
So, when a man goes with mangoes and I,
Go in the Aygo, the mangoes don't go,
In the tacos, nachos, tomatoes, potatoes,
Dough, avocados, Creme fraiche, oregano.
So when there's nowhere for the mangoes to go,
It's: "please go man with the mangoes, man, go."

But where does a man go with a kilo of mangoes
he owns,
When no mangoes go in the tacos we forgo?
Well if a man knows mangoes and tacos don't
go,
Then the mango cargo's embargoed.
For if man grows mangoes in mangroves,
And no man goes where mangoes go,

And mangoes go where no man goes,
Then it just goes to shows that we now know,
When man goes mangoes man goes: no.

Antigua

A holiday was needed, it is true,
So to the Caribbean, we set off.
It was desired after the travel blues,
From days we were stuck home due to a cough.
The moment we arrived and saw the cats,
I knew it would be a place that we'd love.
We chilled by the pool and had lovely chats,
The warmth shining down from high up above.
Highlight: swimming with turtles in the sea,
Bonding over scares while watching Squid
Game.
Gorgeous weather over 30 degrees,
Many cute pictures to fill up our frames.
The food was delicious, so was the rum,
No holiday has ever been so fun!

There's a stream

There's a stream,
Down over the path,
And through the woods,
Just shy of the fields,
And bordered by mud

A slippery, shiny eel,
Of melting glass flows,
Molten silver dancing,
Down over the path,
It grows

Too shallow for fish,
Too deep for paddling,
But hidden through the woods,
Fit for children,
Imagining

For in these places,
These shabby, tiny Edens,
The whole world shrinks,
Into one blissful dream,
Freeing

And there's a stream,
Down over the path,
And through the woods,
Just shy of the field,
And bordered by mud

Take me there,
I'll take you there too,
It can be our place forever,
Just me and you.

Kit and Holly

The spiders are crawling,
On bell jars and window panes,
Heady sunlight bleaching,
Rusted bonnet and blood stains,
A hard brake and screeching,
The dust over empty plains

A red strawy head of hair,
Dainty dress in brightest blue,
Boyish smile, vacant stare,
A pair of schoolgirl's shoes,
Secrets on the roof of her mouth,
Spelling out all that she knew

Denim coat and jeans,
Scuffed-up cowboy boots,
Foot on the pedal,
Bullet holes from hot pursuits,
Powder burns and screams,
All turned down to mute

Now a gun weighs heavy,
In his garbage man's hands,
Cut-throat, nerves steady,
The deadly dreamer's last stand,

Bloody spilt already,
Across the listless badlands.

Miracle

The littlest of toes,
And Scrabble tile smiles,
Milky white eyes,
And all, all of the time.

Which star did they cut her out of?

"Which star did they cut her out of?" I asked,
For her very outline is pure sunshine,
The hopping, skipping, jumping joy of May,
And the cool, moony blues of winter nights,
A dancing, flowing dress, rippling on grass,
Below the golden wind-blows of her hair,
And the untempered smile of mid-laughter,
Lighting up the entire world around her,
So perhaps there's no one star, after all,
For when I look at her, it's every star,
Not one or two, that glistens in her smile,
She's the whole night sky brought from the
heavens,
The brightest silver fairy lights that I,
Hold tight, until forever passes by.

Sally's poem

Faces pass by on the trains of the Metro,
People move past the greys of the street,
Offices open and empty with the light and the
dark,
Bars live and die with the happy and the sad,
But always there, the girl on the table,
Far from home, but home in her thoughts,
Living each second to forget the seconds around
it,
And old Paris stays locked away in the heart of a
dream.

My love

Kobe, my teammate,
Our story will never end,
The love of my life.

Across the world in just one day

In a dozy airport lounge,
There were people watching, waiting
behind suitcases and excited smiles.
The air was filled with expectation
And the smell of coffee from crushed paper
cups.
Excitement and worry in equal measure,
A child's clenched fist and the reassurance of his
mother.
The minutes dragged on for what seemed like
forever,
The quiet anticipation, the coming of adventure.
"How big is the world, really?" He asked.
With the runway before them, she realised and
said:
"It's as big as we make it,
Growing each time with all that we find."
He stopped and thought and smiled,
It's boarding in five.

Sunflower eyes

A cut-crystal arrowhead,
With a twinkle in its eye,
A disco ball necklace,
Scatters walls with light,
Diamonds and gems jewel her smile,
A sparkling starlight cuts through the night

Those winking blue polka dots,
Those tiny black specks,
Pupily raindrops,
Of spectacle lens,
A spinning top of turquoise never to stop,
Her sunflower eyes will never grow old.

New places

New places, new lights, new scenes,
Are all consuming in my dreams.

New places, new names, new drives,
Constantly enrich our lives.

New places, new walks, new streets,
The challenges are no small feat.

New places, new views, new sights,
Exciting in the world's delights.

New places, new fun, new truths,
Are only so special when I'm with you.

Organ pipes

Tell me it's not real,
That it's fake, that it's faulty,
An organ pipe screams,
And it rattles the churchyard,
The crescent moon's sharper,
Than bayonets in crossfire,
The tree branches stretch,
And they ache and they gather,
Scratching the windows,
With fingers like daggers,
And leaving their nail marks,
Down pictures of Jesus,
And trying to widen,
The distance between us

So tell me it's fake,
And tell me it's faulty
And tell me it's fake,
And tell me it's faulty,
And tell me it's fake,
And tell me it's faulty,
And tell me it's fake,
And tell me it's faulty,
I'm fake and I'm faulty

Longing

Days pass by
like the waxing and waning of the moon.
The patterns we tread,
Always too much but never enough.
Desire fills our souls
But we seldom act upon those dreams.
Boredom consumes
When we have so many moments to savour.
Yet everything we truly need,
Is there within our daily lives:
Love and hope,
Joy and security,
What more could we ask for?
So why are we always longing for more?

Tuck me in

A blanket-like quiet,
Shatters upon touch,
Cloak me in its shards,
And turn off the light.

Sickly blue

There's arms in the mattress, I swear,
Writhing about and holding me down,
They won't let me out,
There's arms in the mattress: despair.

Wide Asleep

A dancing kaleidoscope,
Of a rainbow mosaic,
Blown into a million pieces

Reds, blues, greens,
Yellows, oranges, purples,
Scattered across sunbeams,
Into tiny, shiny, glassy,
Reels of fabrics, of dreams,
Unwound, unravelled, unbound,
Unfurled into a flip book,
Of polaroids and memories,
A scrapbook leaking out,
Of the mind's eye, half-shut,
Blinking in the dust,
Of the detritus of stars

I wake.

Four footprints

With her, there's two, along this path,
Through tangled weeds, dull moods,
Bad dreams

Though often it seems not so,
There's two on this path with her, you know,
For while it all seems awful dark,
And laughs and smiles are far apart,
It's all the brighter for knowing now,
There's two that walk the path, with her

So hard it feels to know there's more,
Beyond the portholes of my skull,
A swash of faceless faces,
No knowledge, none, of who they are,
No inkling, guess, of who they'll be,
To be alone it always feels,
Until she walks the path with me

In darkest nights, the path can fork,
Tree fingers reaching out,
But the path does call, not far away,
For she does walk it too

And while there seems no guarantee,
That how I feel is what you see,
That where I walk is where you'll be,
The path is always lit by you,
Four footprints, not by two.